1996 DATE DUE

KIDS
In and Out of
TROUBLE

KIDS
In and Out of
TROUBLE

Margaret O. Hyde

Cobblehill Books
Dutton New York

For Pierre Sayad, M.D.

Library of Congress Cataloging-in-Publication Data
Hyde, Margaret O. (Margaret Oldroyd), date
    Kids in and out of trouble / Margaret O. Hyde.
        p.   cm.
    Includes bibliographical references and index.
    ISBN 0-525-65149-7
    1. Juvenile delinquency—United States—Juvenile litera-
ture. 2. Juvenile justice, Administration of—United States—
Juvenile literature.   I. Title.   HV9104.H95   1995
364.3'6'0973—dc20   94-16617   CIP

Published in the United States by Cobblehill Books,
an affiliate of Dutton Children's Books,
a division of Penguin Books USA Inc.
375 Hudson Street, New York, New York 10014

Designed by Joseph Rutt
Printed in the United States of America
First Edition   10 9 8 7 6 5 4 3 2 1

ACKNOWLEDGMENTS

The author wishes to thank the many individuals and organizations who contributed to this book. Troubled teens, counselors, and many young people who work to help others were especially helpful.

Contents

CHAPTER ONE

KIDS IN TROUBLE:
Everyone's Problem

A fourteen-year-old boy was seriously injured today when a classmate stabbed him in the back. No one could explain how the weapon, probably a knife, passed the school's metal detectors. The victim is listed in serious condition, after undergoing surgery for a punctured lung." This case made the papers because the weapon escaped detection.

"Three people were killed last night in a drive-by shooting as they walked toward a pizza parlor. The fifteen-year-old murderer, who was apprehended two blocks away, told police he just felt like shooting someone. His assault rifle lay on the front seat of the car when the police captured him. He made no effort to resist arrest. He told police they could not do much to him because he was a juvenile."

The list of crimes committed by kids is long and varied. Even though a large percentage of young people are not involved in criminal activity, teens and children are committing more murders and other serious crime than ever before. And no matter where you live, the problem of kids in trouble with the law affects you. Perhaps you know someone who has been arrested, or someone who takes risks that may lead to violence and crime. Perhaps you have even become an innocent victim.

Kids are in trouble for many reasons: drugs, poverty, homelessness, gangs, violence at home, in school, and on the streets. What is being done about it? Juvenile justice systems throughout the United States are overburdened and underfunded. They were created to rehabilitate young offenders, but are they getting the job done? Can they rehabilitate someone who has grown into his or her teens without education, proper nutrition, learning in moral responsibility and any career skills or hope for the future? Arguments rage over how tough the juvenile justice system should be, but unless enough people take an interest in it, there will be little action.

The advocates of harsh punishment and those who want to attack the root causes of juvenile crime agree that crime is a real crisis in America. Many experts are moving toward making young violent offenders accountable for their acts. And many agree that most crimes can be traced to the early stages in a child's life. They look to families, schools, religion, and the media to help in moral training. Blacks are searching for answers to the violent crimes of black on black. The problem is complex, and help is needed from every possible source.

The majority of young people do try to stay out of trouble and work toward a hopeful future. In spite of the alarming numbers of troubled kids, a great many manage to show responsibility, self-respect, and find avenues other than crime to attain their goals. And a number of young people have found ways to help other kids in trouble, and ways to decrease the violence.

It is time for teens everywhere to take a look at what is happening to their generation, to be aware of how many live in an atmosphere of crime and violence. Knowing about some of the causes of crime, how kids are treated when they are arrested, and what efforts are being made to prevent juvenile crime is a beginning in making the world safer for tomorrow.

Almost everyone agrees that prevention is a good way to attack a problem, and that it is the ultimate hope for reducing juvenile delinquency. Young people themselves are helping to make this happen. While some kids are just trying to survive in the communities where the streets are growing meaner, others are looking for ways to decrease the violence. Many young people are doing something to help kids stay out of trouble with the law. Do you want to be one of them?

CHAPTER TWO

JUVENILE CRIME:
The Changing Scene

Young people are committing more murders and other serious crimes than ever before, but the number who are involved has not grown. Delbert S. Elliott, Director of the Center for the Study and Prevention of Violence at the University of Colorado, believes that most juvenile crime is being committed by about 6 percent of the young. But these kids seem to get tougher. They have become more violent in recent years.

Violence makes the headlines, fills the television screens, and the streets of many cities, some of which have become known as war zones. In a culture that continues to glorify and glamorize violence, the problem of how to prevent juvenile crime and how to help kids in trouble has grown to overwhelming proportions. About one-quarter, or seven million, of today's adolescents are at serious risk of falling prey to alcohol and other illegal drugs, teenage pregnancy, educational problems, violence, and death, according to Fred Hechinger, author of *Fateful Choices: Healthy Youth for the 21st Century*. What does this mean for the world of tomorrow? What does this mean for your world? Can you make a difference?

While there are no easy answers, people, both young and old, cannot afford to ignore the stresses and dangers that many young people face today. America's children, in all ethnic groups and at all income levels, have been called "children in crisis." This is especially true for blacks. Black men between the ages of fifteen and twenty-four are murdered at ten times the national average. But young blacks are speaking out against the large numbers of black men who are killing each other, and pointing out that the vast majority of blacks are law-abiding citizens.

Organizations which study the well-being of children are speaking out about the conditions of all the young today, citing problems for rich and poor. There are drops in academic achievement, an ever-widening breakup of families, increased violence in music and on television, and for the poor, the major risk factors that lead to problem behavior are even worse than for children raised in safe neighborhoods.

About 2.3 million persons under the age of eighteen are arrested by law enforcement agencies in the United States each year, according to the Office of Juvenile Justice and Delinquency Prevention. There are far more murders, rapes, and robberies by young people than in the past. The number of arrests of persons under the age of eighteen for violent crimes increased 62 percent between 1986 and 1991. Not all such crimes resulted in arrest, but there are other indicators of an increasing and changing crime scene among the young. For example, a 1993 survey by the National School Safety Council reports that 100,000 students across the country bring guns to school each day. Some of these students say that they do so for self-protection, but even their guns can cause tragedy.

Consider the case of a student, who reached in his backpack for a book, accidentally discharged his gun and killed a classmate. In one recent year, the increase in the number of guns confiscated from students in the Los Angeles Unified School District was 86 percent. Since 1965, the arrest rate for juveniles charged with violent crime has more than tripled.

Not only is the number of violent crimes increasing, the age of the offenders is decreasing. Ten-year-olds break into neighbors' houses; a pair of twelve- and fifteen-year-olds tie a man to a tree and set him on fire; a twelve-year-old murders a classmate in a fight over a baseball. These are just a few examples that illustrate the changing nature of juvenile crime.

In 1994, homicide was the third-leading cause of death for elementary and middle school children. In *Saving Our Kids from Delinquency, Drugs and Despair*, Falcon Baker suggests that crime is no longer a young man's game; it's getting to be child's play. Games of cops and robbers are now played with real guns, not toys.

Consider the games some teens play today in areas that are considered safe. Stealing cars is one. In a wealthy suburban area where the odor of burned rubber permeates the air on Saturday nights, citizens complain that teens have etched eights and doughnuts on the asphalt roads with the tires of their stolen cars. These kids lead less dangerous lives than many in urban areas, but they, too, seem unconcerned about the risk of dying. To them, the risk of dying in a car crash adds to the thrill of car theft. Some of their friends are held in jails after injuring or killing people who happened to be in the way. But most of these teens feel that it will not happen to them.

"Carjacking" is a new name for an old, but popular, teen crime. The players in this violent game steal a car by threatening the driver with a gun, forcing him or her to get out of the car. These thieves drive away while the owners of the cars stand in the street in a state of shock. Many carjackers act in daylight in places as crowded as a supermarket parking lot. In one case, the ejected driver was caught in the car door and carried along, her body bumping along the road as the car sped forward. People have been killed for resisting, or just for not getting out of their cars fast enough.

Although there have always been crimes by juveniles that appear to lack a motive, there seem to be more senseless crimes. For example, young people tried to set fire to homeless men sleeping in subway stations as many as twenty-two times in 1992. In these crimes, no one takes anything of value; there is nothing to take. The victims all appeared to be strangers to their torturers. One fire setter explained that he and his friends were playing near a man who was sleeping in the subway and they accidentally spilled some of their rum on him. Then they threw matches at him and when his blanket caught fire, they ran. Two other homeless men, who happened to come along soon after the fire started, threw themselves on the man and smothered the flames. They called the police, and ran after the boys. At the police station, the boys were charged with assault and attempted murder. They gave no good reasons for the attempts, although the fun of it was suggested as a motive.

Almost everyone agrees that many young criminals are becoming more violent. The number of murderers under the age of eighteen has climbed 93 percent over the last decade. Murder is more common among today's children, many of whom are in trouble because of the violence around them. The Children's Defense Fund, a nonprofit organization supported primarily by foundations, corporate grants, and individual donations, reports that two children under the age of five are murdered in America each day. In the same short period of time, about 7,000 children are reported abused or neglected. Many more cases are not reported.

Growing up in America today is different for most young people than it was for their parents. Fear of violence and crime seems to be everywhere, from the mean streets of large cities to the halls of suburban and rural schools. Teenage boys, who once fought over their places in the drug market, now shoot so readily that the reasons may be only sneakers, leather jackets, or insults. Bystanders are caught in the cross fire of drug wars and people can be shot just because a young person feels like killing someone. Some kids have become so desensitized to shooting that they laugh about it. On the streets in many cities, "doing time" is a badge of honor.

Many adults are not, or do not want to be, aware of what is happening to today's children. They move farther from the cities, believing they can escape the problems of children in trouble. But even conservative magazines, that usually devote their pages more to business than social problems, are printing articles about today's "children in crisis." For example, in one issue of *Forbes* magazine, boys and girls from different cities talk about violence, hopes, cops, racism, drugs, school, and family. Others talk about juvenile homicide, suicide, and abuse.

The Committee for Economic Development reflects the views of corporate America when it states publicly that it is concerned about whether or not children of today will have sufficient education, motivations, and undamaged brains to provide the needs of tomorrow's labor force.

In addition to being more numerous and more serious, crimes by and to the young have changed in character. Boys used to settle arguments with their fists; now they settle them with guns. Gang members were once armed with zip guns; now they carry machine guns. Not long ago, kids were considered hopelessly delinquent when they skipped a day of school, stole an apple from the grocer, broke a window, or went joyriding one evening in the family car without permission. Today, many juveniles sell drugs, rape, rob, and shoot to kill.

Most boys and girls go through a period of antisocial behavior, or rule breaking, as they find their separate identities in the growing-up process; they revolt against parental or community rules in ways that are not violent. Even today, most young people grow up healthy, hopeful, and able to meet the challenges of adult life. A relatively few become involved with the law for offenses that vary from vandalism to murder, but the number who do are creating an atmosphere of fear.

Many voices are being raised in protest to the revolving doors of juvenile justice systems, where young people are arrested but released, only to be arrested soon again. A ten-year-old can be a lookout for adult criminals and know that he will not be seriously punished if he is caught.

While some child advocates are calling for the rights of the child, others are trying to address the problem of community violence by building more prisons and making tougher sentences for those who stand trial. What do you think should be done?

Large numbers of kids in poor areas feel that they have nothing to lose. Too many are growing up with a lack of feelings. They grow up unable to trust, love, and make meaningful relationships with other people. Many have been abused and will abuse their children.

Many of today's young already resort to drugs and brutality in an effort to get a sense of their own existence and to numb the deadness inside. Suppose a child lives in ten different homes before he starts kindergarten. He is farmed out to relatives, until they have no more room for him. Then he goes into foster care, and he is moved three times in one year. He always seems unhappy, refuses to abide by family rules, and never seems to develop a sense of attachment to any adult. Foster mothers of such children often complain that they seem like sticks when picked up. They do not throw their arms around their mothers when they are hugged, the way most children do. They remain aloof, and even many of those who are lucky enough to live with firm but loving foster mothers may go through life without feeling the emotions necessary to find love and happiness. Even though they try drugs and crime to feel alive, they feel no guilt.

Consider the case of three boys who raped a woman in a park. One, during questioning at the police station, said he was the good guy because he put her pocketbook under her head to make her more comfortable. He saw nothing wrong in what he had done. He, and many like him, will continue to prey on the public and to commit serious violent crimes. Attempts to rehabilitate them appear futile. This boy and thousands like him are in trouble, and the search is on for solutions that will help prevent the increase in the number of unattached, unfeeling children who are creating such terror. There are no simple answers, but there may be ways to help prevent many such problems.

The fear of violence by the young is changing the lives of people everywhere. In a world where the young have easy access to guns and no access to the American dream of success, anyone can be the victim of a shoot-out. Many thirteen-year-olds have attended more funerals for their friends than for grandparents. No wonder many young adults are pleading with political leaders and the general public to address some of the causes of violent crime: drugs, poverty, guns, and a value system that seems to make no sense. They plead for a new look at an antiquated juvenile justice system that is overwhelmed with cases and sometimes sends young people back to the streets with more desire and ability to break the law than before they entered the system.

What kind of system can cope with today's world in which many children have nightmares in the daytime, have mothers on crack, are abused by their natural parents, go to bed hungry, don't know their fathers, and who may die from gunshot wounds before they reach their tenth birthday? What can help kids who are growing up without love or affection, without beliefs, with no value for life? What can be done to make progress toward giving children a healthy and fair start in life?

According to the Honorable Charles D. Gill of Litchfield, Connecticut, the nation is in grave danger because of its benign neglect of its only real national treasure—its children. Many young people agree and they are looking for ways to make a difference in their world where violent death is the second leading cause of death for boys and more than four out of ten girls become pregnant at least once in their teens.

Whether out of compassion for others or concern for the world of tomorrow, there is a call to action. Ideas about how to keep kids out of trouble with the law differ. Some people believe that getting tougher with delinquents will help to break the cycle of violence and crime. While many people see delinquency as a result of poverty, racial discrimination, children having children, changes in family structure, poor health, illiteracy, lack of hope, and an environment of drugs and violence, they are searching for solutions. An increasing number of advocates are pushing for rights for kids, citing the many cases in which the young suffer from parental abuse and have no way out of their terrible situations.

According to Judge David B. Mitchell, associate judge of Baltimore, Maryland, City Circuit Court, "It is of no value for the court to work miracles in rehabilitation if there are no opportunities for the child in the community and if the child is simply going to return to the squalor from which he or she came."

Judge Mitchell believes that most juvenile institutions are simply little prisons where inmates make contacts for future criminal activities. "For one of the first times in our Nation's history," he says, "we have a permanent under-class of poor black, white and Hispanic kids. These kids see no opportunities. They reside in intense, comprehensive poverty, have inadequate housing and educational systems that do not function. Until we deal with the environment in which kids live, whatever we do in the courts is irrelevant."

Many rural kids are in trouble, too. "A higher rate of kids in rural environments use tobacco, and alcohol in binge drinking, than kids in urban environments. Unless we recognize that substance abuse affects all of America and start attacking the broad scope of the problem, the juvenile court, the criminal court, and all courts will be irrelevant. All we shall be is conductors on the railroad to prison."

Unless there is increased awareness of what is happening in the world of juvenile crime, there is little hope for solutions through prevention. Even though progress in the war on juvenile crime may be measured in inches, you may be able to make a small difference.

CHAPTER THREE

CHILDREN IN TROUBLE LONG AGO

There have always been children in trouble with the law. Although some of the ways that such kids are treated today seem especially cruel, consider what happened through the years and how the justice system progressed.

"In criminal cases, an infant at the age of fourteen may be capitally punished for any capital offense, but under the age of seven he cannot. The period between seven and fourteen is subject to much uncertainty. . . . If he could discern between good and evil at the time of the offense committed, he may be convicted and receive judgment and execution of death though he hath not attained to years of puberty or discretion."

The above appeared on the records in London about

the middle of the eighteenth century. Although it was not a common occurrence, children were hanged for taking the lives of others. The public believed that sparing a child because of tender years would set a bad example and might be of dangerous consequence to the public.

The juvenile justice system, which began in the United States in 1898, took a different approach. It began as a humane effort to protect children in trouble from harsh treatment, and its ideals were lofty. However, not all went as planned. Today, the juvenile justice system is often called the "juvenile injustice system," but the treatment of children before it began was even worse. Many children, who committed minor crimes, were tried in adult courts and sentenced to the same prisons as adults. Some died on the same gallows as older criminals.

From earliest times, childhood was completely lacking in any form of social justice. Children were the property of parents who considered them as small adults. Babies were dressed in swaddling clothes, perhaps to keep them from interfering with the lives of adults, although it may have been thought to keep their bodies in a position that would make them grow straight, or for other reasons. In any case, babies were not prized as they are today. As they grew older, they became part of the labor force, helping their parents on farms and in cottage industries, such as shoemaking, spinning yarn, producing pots and pans and other needed items. Children, on the whole, were exploited, ignored, and mistreated.

Since the concepts of childhood and adolescence did

not emerge until well into the nineteenth century, it is not surprising to find that most adults did not give serious thought to the welfare of their children. Boys and girls were considered miniature adults, or peculiar unformed animals, with a status somewhere between that of slaves and animals. Many children were physically and sexually abused, sold into slavery, murdered, left to die, and even brutally maimed so that they would be more successful beggars.

Even as ideas about children began to change to ones of interest and concern, young lawbreakers were still treated harshly. In the eighteenth century, spankings for minor offenses were so hard that they would be considered beatings in today's world. Many of the children who committed serious crimes were thrown into prisons, disfigured and hanged, much as adults were.

In eighteenth-century England, some children who committed crimes were put aboard ships and transported to prison colonies in Australia. Imagine the agony of children as young as eleven being torn from their families to endure a difficult sea voyage that was followed by life in a strange land. In this same century, children in England were frequently removed from their prison cells to live on abandoned and rotting ships that served as offshore prisons.

In the eighteenth and nineteenth centuries, the harsh treatment of children in trouble with the law aroused the sympathy of many men who became reformers, both in England and in the United States. For example, when some men learned about records that showed about five hundred children were in Newgate Prison in London between 1813 and 1817, they were appalled. These children were mixed with the general prison population and had no special care. The crimes of which they were guilty were, in some cases, as petty as the stealing of a loaf of bread by a hungry child.

Among the attempts that were made by various groups of adults who wanted to make life better for young criminals was the formation of the Philanthropic Society in London in 1788. In the beginning, the society aimed to help children of prisoners by removing them from "evil company." Later, young "criminals" were helped. Records show that one boy, who had stolen a watch, was rescued from living with a mixture of criminals, many of whom were violent adults. But, in spite of these noble efforts, comparatively few children were protected by the Society. Many hundreds continued to be confined in prisons. No one knows the full extent of mistreatment.

Through the years, many other attempts were made to change the treatment of children who had broken the law. One resulted in the establishment of the first institution in the United States for juvenile delinquents. This was the House of Refuge, built in New York City in 1825. James W. Gerard, who played a large part in establishing it, had defended a boy who was accused of stealing a bird. He argued that prison would corrupt the boy. After he investigated the conditions for other children in prisons, he and Isaac Collins, a Quaker, helped to release many children from adult prisons to the new House of Refuge.

Efforts to subdue youth with kindness were planned, but treatment at the House of Refuge was often harsh. Children were to be employed every day of the year, except Sundays, since the prevention of idleness was expected to lead to reform. Punishments for disobedience were severe. They ranged from loss of play periods, or being sent to bed without supper, to being forced to drink a bitter herb tea which caused a child to sweat profusely. Serious offenders were put in solitary confinement, whipped, and put in irons. All of this was considered a step forward in the treatment of juvenile offenders from the way they were treated in adult prisons, perhaps because they were no longer ignored or beaten by adult prisoners.

In those days, a juvenile offender could be any child who had broken the law, who wandered about the streets when he or she should have been in school or at work, and lacked "good family." Running away, staying out of school without permission, begging, and prostitution were added to the crimes of theft, violence, and destruction.

During the nineteenth century, a number of reform, or training schools, emerged as adults became more aware of the need to separate children from adults in prisons. However, many of these were not much better than the prisons. Later in the century, an increasing number of reformers began to work toward more lenient treatment in the hope of saving children from a life of crime.

Perhaps the most famous case that opened the eyes of Americans to the plight of children was that of Mary Ellen

Kids In and Out of Trouble

Wilson. In 1874, Mary Ellen lived with her adoptive parents in a New York City apartment. This eight-year-old girl was held there in chains, beaten, and starved. Her screams aroused neighbors, who made many calls to the police, but the police took no action because they could not interfere with a family affair. A child was the property of parents, who could treat her as they wished. Some concerned neighbors and church workers were able to rescue Mary Ellen through the help of the Society for the Protection of Animals. They made it clear that Mary Ellen was technically an animal, and she could legally be removed from her home. By the time this happened, she was so weak she had to be carried out of the apartment on a stretcher.

After learning that dogs and cats could be protected from abuse while children could not, many groups were formed to protect children. Only a small percentage of the abused and neglected were reached, but now there were places to go for help.

In addition to being beaten and neglected, many children of the nineteenth century spent long hours working in factories, mills, mines, and on farms. New labor and education laws were gradually introduced by government, private, and religious agencies, but many children still suffered from maltreatment at home. Many still do, even though laws have been passed to protect them.

Along with the unrest about the treatment of children during the second half of the nineteenth century, the concept of a special court for juveniles was born. Women's groups played a major role in this, for the women felt that the young boys and girls, who were still being exploited in factories and sweatshops, were apt to fall into a life of stealing and other crimes. Pressure from the Chicago Women's Club, along with general dissatisfaction with the institutions that dealt with young offenders, led to the establishment of the first juvenile court system to help "little offenders along their rough paths." The Illinois Juvenile Court Act became law on July 1, 1899, and at that time, children were no longer tried as adults. However, today there is a tendency toward trying an increasing number of young violent offenders as adults.

In 1905, the Illinois Juvenile Court Act was amended to include a long list of children they were to deal with. A delinquent was a child "who is incorrigible" or one who "is growing up in idleness and crime." Children who would not obey their parents, the poor, immigrants, vagrants, those who were found "habitually begging" or "playing musical instruments" on the streets could be considered delinquent.

The Illinois juvenile court system was the basis for the entire juvenile justice system. In 1909, in Pennsylvania, the law directed the courts to consider the child as one in need of care and protection of the state, not as one on trial for the commission of a crime. By 1910, there were juvenile courts in most states, with the philosophy that juveniles could not be considered criminals.

The "best interest of the child" was to be considered, something that could not be accomplished if children were placed with adult criminals. Delinquent children were to be rescued, not punished, with the judge acting as the wise father the child probably did not have. A child was not considered to be on trial for the commission of a crime, but was supposed to have the care and protection of the state. This was also true for abused and neglected children who found their way into the system in Illinois and throughout the United States.

In 1966, there was a major change in this system that was not supposed to find guilt, or to punish, but must try to rehabilitate. Considerable attention arose from the case of Morris A. Kent, Jr., who was obviously a kid in trouble. He had been arrested for housebreaking and purse snatching in 1959 and put on probation. Two years later, he was arrested for entering a woman's apartment, robbing and raping her. He admitted to the robbery and the rape, and volunteered information about some other robberies and rapes. His mother provided him with a lawyer who wanted to plead insanity, but there were no hearings. Kent, as many others before him, did not fit the picture of the innocent, misguided child who could be rehabilitated by the kindly parent, the state. The judge waived jurisdiction and sent Kent to criminal court to be tried as an adult. This case called into question whether or not the court could fulfill its part in being the kindly parent without resorting to due process, the procedure which protects a person from being deprived of life, liberty, or property without reasonable and lawful procedures.

Although Kent was tried in adult court, given a thirty-to-ninety-year sentence for robbery, was found guilty of rape "by reason of insanity" and committed to a mental hospital to serve out this sentence, the sentence was appealed. This case made its way to the Supreme Court and was the first case in which this court considered juvenile procedures. The sentence was dismissed on the grounds of irregularity in the way it was handled.

In 1967, the way the juvenile court system dealt with kids in trouble was called into question by another case. A fifteen-year-old boy, Gerald Gault, was arrested after being charged with making an obscene phone call to a neighbor. Without letting his parents know of the charge against him, he was placed in a juvenile detention home. Gerald had previously been involved in two cases that involved the police: one time he was questioned about the stealing of a baseball glove, and one time he was found to be in the company of a boy who stole a wallet. In the case of the phone call, no attempt was made to prove whether or not he actually made the call. Gerald's mother requested that the neighbor who made the report be brought to his hearing so that her testimony could be challenged. This was not done. The judge sentenced Gerald to the state industrial school until he reached the age of twenty-one, unless he was discharged sooner by due process of law. When questioned about the sentence, the judge said he thought the boy was delinquent on the basis of his being involved in immoral matters.

Gerald's case was only one of many that did not fulfill the purpose of the juvenile system in which the state was to act as a loving, firm parent who acted in the best interest of the child, but it became famous because it reached the Supreme Court. Gerald would have received better treatment if he had been proved guilty when he was over eighteen years of age. Then he would have been tried as an adult and imprisoned for no more than two months or fined $50 or less.

The Gault case is known as a landmark case because it made it clear that juveniles have a right to adequate representation by an attorney, the right to be properly notified of the charges, and the right to confront and cross-examine witnesses.

In 1970, the Supreme Court went a step further. It ruled that the guilt of juveniles had to be proved without a reasonable doubt. More attention was now being paid to the rights of children.

In 1974, The Juvenile Justice and Delinquency Prevention Act was passed and money was allotted for a wide variety of programs. One of the major purposes was to remove the so-called status offenders from the system. Status offenders are children who are "unruly and beyond control," and children who violate laws which do not apply to adults. Even today, if you skip school or disobey a curfew law, you would be classed as a status offender.

Through the next few years, the court realized there was a need for the protection of the community as well as the needs and best interest of the child. As violent crime increased, the number of juveniles referred to adult court grew. But so did the number of cases in juvenile courts.

If the juvenile justice system is to be a fair one, it cannot function with the overwhelming number of cases it must handle. Today, there are too many offenders in the courtroom and too few ideas about how to deal with them. There are many experts and other people who are involved with the system who say it is an injustice system. Many people feel that there should be a return to the concept of responsibility and punishment for crimes, no matter what the age of a person. Almost everyone agrees that there is a need for change to help kids in trouble and to protect society from the violent offenders.

CHAPTER FOUR

ARRESTED: What Happens Now?

T hey can't do anything to me. I'm a juvenile," is a popular comment in communities where feelings of self-worth come from crime.

Most kids who break the law never become involved in the juvenile justice system because they are not caught. Others, who commit minor crimes, are released because authorities feel that they have a better chance of becoming good citizens if they are just reprimanded and allowed to return to their families without becoming part of the system where they may remain for years of attempted rehabilitation.

What happens when a kid is arrested depends somewhat on where he or she lives. Some state statutes define arrested youth as adults and handle them through the adult criminal system rather than through a juvenile justice system. In some states, only serious juvenile offenses, such as murder, are handled by the adult court, while in others, these offenders remain in the juvenile system.

A state's juvenile system may serve its purpose well in some cases, but in other cases in the same state, a serious offense may be treated much too lightly and a trivial offense much too seriously. Many criminologists and sociologists say that the juvenile justice system has collapsed under the weight of its charge to rehabilitate the young who have broken the law.

Since the juvenile justice system is not just one system, laws vary from place to place and from time to time. Even the age at which a person is considered to be a juvenile varies. In most states, a juvenile is a person under the age of eighteen. Once the juvenile court has jurisdiction, he or she may remain under the court's supervision until the age of twenty-one in most states, and even longer in others.

There are judges who feel that it is important to concentrate on older offenders, while others feel that it is more important to concentrate on the young. Many authorities who study delinquency say kids in the eight-to-twelve-year-old range are more likely to become dangerous delinquents and adult criminals than the older delinquents, who appear in court for the first time as a result of rebelling against authority in the process of growing up. They emphasize prevention through teaching responsibility at an early age.

Kids In and Out of Trouble

Judges have little time to explore each case, for their calendars are jammed. Picture a judge in juvenile court, or family court, as it is called in some places, rushing through her daily schedule. The courtroom is filled with people carrying out various duties, and there is confusion because of breakdowns in old equipment and lack of enough equipment and personnel. A fifteen-year-old boy comes before the judge for a drug offense and the papers show that he has been arrested several times before. The judge has no time to delve into his family situation, one in which there has been abuse and neglect. She notes that the boy is surly and appears uncaring. She bases her opinion partly on his attitude, on the number of times the boy has been arrested, and the nature of his current misbehavior, that of possession of marijuana. The boy is sent to a training camp, where he is supposed to be rehabilitated and returned to society with a better concern for right and wrong. He may be forced to stay there until he reaches the age of adulthood in his state.

The next case that comes before the judge is one in which a boy has held a knife at the throat of an older boy after being tortured verbally and physically. He tells the judge that the older boy had threatened to kill him and he was just protecting himself. His former record is good, he appears sincere, and his lawyer presents the boy in a favorable light. The judge decides to give the boy a chance by placing him on probation, even though his offense was serious.

In the case that follows, a boy has stolen a thousand

dollars worth of a neighbor's silver in order to pay for cocaine. His parents replaced the silver as soon as they learned what happened, and the neighbor is willing to drop the charges. The parents have made it known that they will see that their son enters a drug treatment program or will see a therapist so that he will "become a good citizen." These parents, and many like them, keep their promises for several weeks, but they become so busy with their own lives that their son is soon free to do as he pleases. Drug use continues, and the boy is eventually arrested again. His delinquency increases and he thinks juvenile court is a joke. He acts bored at the hearings, and brags that the chances of anything serious happening to him are slight. He may be right.

Are the juvenile judges, who give only a few minutes to each case, at fault? They have to hear a long list of cases each day in order to clear their calendars so that juveniles being held for court appearances do not wait beyond the time allowed by law. Unfortunately, the time a juvenile spends in lockup awaiting his or her brief time in court varies from overnight to months, even though laws may specify this period must be shorter. When the juvenile does reach the court, the judges have usually not had time to find out the real story behind each crime. They have few places to send the offenders. Most just do the best they can.

Many difficult things can happen in the name of justice, even for the same offense. About half of the cases may be handled informally by the arresting officer, with offenders being released without becoming part of the system, or its statistics. This is especially true in the case of status offenses, acts for which an adult would not be prosecuted (possession of alcohol, truancy, running away from home). However, in another court, the boy or girl may be detained.

According to a report by the United States Department of Justice, one in five runaway youths nationwide were admitted to secure detention facilities while their cases were being processed by the court. In one state, 11 percent were detained, but in another as many as 60 percent were detained.

Many police departments are in agreement with the critics who feel that a child has less chance of becoming a delinquent if he or she can be kept out of the system. No one knows how many cases are dismissed without being reported. This helps the offender, but it also gives many kids the idea that they will be released for any crime because they are juveniles. Even though a juvenile may be considered a victim of his or her environment, there is a trend toward making young offenders do penance. More and more pressure is building among authorities to make juveniles accountable for their actions. More resources are needed for judges so that the offender does not perceive that he or she has a "free ride," but is not incarcerated for an overly long period of time.

According to the January, 1993, Federal Register, which is published daily by the United States Government Printing Office, nearly two-thirds of the juvenile offenders who were actually taken into custody were referred by police to juvenile courts. Only about one in a hundred of the juveniles arrested goes to a correctional institution. Cases are often dismissed for lack of evidence, or because the court feels that there is no need for further intervention.

Separating juvenile offenders from hardened criminals in penal institutions (jails and prisons) and keeping them out of any institution was a major purpose of The Juvenile Justice and Delinquency Prevention Act of 1974. It tried to rehabilitate juveniles by working with the family through the guidance of a person known as a probation officer. To some degree, this is true today.

Cassie was arrested during a rock concert where she became aggressive after drinking too much beer. Although many people at the concert smoked marijuana and crack, the police arrested her because she tossed beer bottles in their direction. She had no drugs, other than alcohol, in her possession. Cassie was taken to the station in a police car, told about the seriousness of her actions, and released in the care of her parents, who promised to get help for her drinking problem. Cassie was never arrested again. If she had been charged formally, taken to court, and placed in a detention center, she might have learned more about breaking the law than she knew before. However, not everyone who breaks a law is dismissed at the police station. And not everyone who goes to a detention center becomes a hardened criminal.

A relatively small number of young people are able to make their terrible experiences in training schools, reform schools, or other institutions work to their advantage. They learn to discipline themselves, to overcome the odds, and mature into good citizens. Waln K. Brown, Director of the William Gladden Foundation, which publishes delinquency prevention materials, is an example of this. He grew up in an impoverished and broken home. As a child, he turned to vagrancy, truancy, and became a difficult juvenile delinquent. His experiences in various institutions were terrible, but he fought his way back to an admirable life-style. He recounts the painful experiences of his troubled years in *The Other Side of Delinquency*, in which he helps professionals to see what is happening to many young people from a juvenile delinquent's point of view. Dr. Brown notes that thousands of delinquents abandon their former way of life and accomplish socially approved adult adjustment. He notes that his pattern of delinquency did not begin overnight, nor did it change quickly. There was no quick cure that magically altered his life. He notes that we know less about how people conquer hardship than about why they are overwhelmed by it. Certainly, some young delinquents are more resilient than others.

In some cases, youths arrested for serious crimes are handled directly through the adult criminal justice system. In others, serious offenders are first referred to the juvenile court system, and may be referred to adult court after their individual cases have been examined.

In juvenile court, each case goes through a number of steps. Intake is the step at which an official of the court collects information about the case, and decides if the offender should be held for a hearing. A date is set for the hearing and the offender appears with a lawyer to represent him or her. At this point, a judge determines whether or not there is probable cause to believe that the specified crime was committed. If the case is not dismissed, another hearing, called a dispositional hearing, is held within the next month or so, depending on individual state laws. At this hearing, the judge decides what will happen to the offender.

Considering the number of cases that pass through juvenile court, the job of dealing with kids in trouble is overwhelming. The nation's juvenile courts disposed of about 1.2 million delinquency cases in 1991, the majority of which involved males. Both kids in trouble and the systems that deal with them need help.

Consider a typical case in which ten-year-old Daren and his friend, fifteen-year-old Mike, sit on the straight chairs of an interrogation room in a police station. While the police are trying to reach their parents, the boys are in the room alone discussing the robbery they have just committed. Daren asks, "What will happen now?" He appears to have mixed feelings about being there. He feels important about committing the crime, for he knows he will gain stature on the street, but he is not sure about how fast he will be able to return home.

Neither Daren nor Mike have any hope of being bailed out. No one in Daren's family will cooperate. Actually, no one in his family cares much about him. His mother is an alcoholic and his father left home when he was a baby.

Kids In and Out of Trouble

Now he has the attention of his friend and the police. For him, this is better than being ignored. Mike is a runaway who lives on the street, and he does not want his parents to know where he is. He has given the police a false address and phone number. There is no chance that anyone will come to rescue him, either.

Daren feels less anxious when Mike assures him that they will be released soon. Mike says, "We might have to go to juvie hall, but they'll probably release us tomorrow. However," he adds, "maybe we'll have to come back to court. They might even send us to rehab camp, or maybe we'll just get probation." Mike wants Daren to believe they'll be back on the street by tomorrow, but he is not so sure.

A number of different things can happen to these two boys. What happens to juveniles who are arrested for a robbery, or any crime, depends on many factors. The enforcement of law in America has always varied in degree and scope. Although many juveniles are just reprimanded by the police, those who are detained for further consideration spend some time in a center that may be called juvenile hall, a reception center, diagnostic clinic, receiving home, or by some other name. To the young who spend time there, it is a juvenile version of a local jail. The fingerprinting and mug shots make the arrest frightening the first time. Many repeat offenders are very casual about it.

Daren remembered the time he was caught stealing cigarettes from the store across from his family's apartment. The police had taken him to the station house and talked with him about the trouble he could be in if he did it again. He was frightened then, but in the next few years, he had stolen a few candy bars from time to time without getting caught. He had heard that most police handle juvenile crime on their own, if the offenses are not serious. Daren was right about this, but he did not realize that "police diversion" often involved releasing kids into parental custody or seeing that the person did some community service.

There were so many kids breaking the law, Mike and Daren felt sure the police would not bother with them. When they stole the money from the newspaper stand, Daren was sure he would not get into much trouble. He did not expect to be one of the more than a million children who are referred to juvenile court each year.

About two-thirds of the cases that go to court are dismissed, or the juvenile is placed in the custody of a parent or guardian. There was not much chance of this happening to Daren, whose mother was not able to care for him, or Mike, who would not contact his parents.

Many of the juvenile offenders are placed on probation and are released with certain restrictions. For example, they must refrain from associating with anyone else on probation or anyone convicted of breaking the criminal law. In many cases, this includes their best friends. Youths on probation must return to school if they are enrolled there, and they must live with their parents, or one parent if this is possible. They cannot enter a place where liquor is served, drive a car, and they must observe a curfew. Breaking probation may mean a return to court, and in some cases a court sentence.

Daren and Mike were given probation. Daren was referred to a social service caseworker who placed him in a foster home. Mike was placed in a halfway house where there was limited security. He was given a full year's probation. Both boys were upset about being separated from each other, but they made new friends. Like most young offenders, there was a chance that they would outgrow their contempt for the law and authority in general. Depending on the situations in which they were placed and their own reactions to them, they might well return to juvenile court.

There are deep differences in the way adults think about what should be done with, or for, young people who break the law. Sometimes it seems as if the laws swing back and forth much like a pendulum on a clock between rehabilitation and punishment. There is a trend toward restitution, a sentence in which the victim works to pay something to the victim of the crime.

One of the most serious problems for today is how the juvenile justice system can really do justice by making offenders responsible for their actions. Many experts are focusing on a person's reaction to his or her environment, rather than what the environment has done to the person.

There is a hard-core group of chronic offenders who will rape and rob with little care for their victims. These kids have never learned how to live in a caring, law-abiding society. They grow up with no conscience, no sense of pity. These are the 6 percent who are responsible for the most violent crimes committed by juveniles. Some exhibit slight concern about their acts, others do not. Many of them, most of whom are boys, have a long history of breaking the law.

Consider the case of twelve-year-old Mickey, who killed an eighty-seven-year-old woman, when she resisted giving up her purse. He cracked her skull with a Coca-Cola bottle. When questioned about him, his mother and lawyer claimed that he did have a conscience, and the social worker reported that he cried one day while talking about the murder. But Mickey grew up on the streets with kids who mugged and had their own sense of what was acceptable behavior. Mickey followed the crowd, and did what the older boys taught him. He had no real sense of what would happen if he went along with a crime of any kind.

Investigations showed that Mickey's mother was a heroin addict and his father, who did not live with the family, stopped by from time to time. The mother had seven children with three different men. She claimed the children drove her to drugs. Mickey lived with brothers, sisters, and a total of twenty family members in the grandmother's home.

Mickey spent much of his time on the streets, where actions seem to have no consequences and many kids are incapable of seeing a relationship between wrong behavior and punishment. Mickey, and the kids who were his role models, did not seem capable of viewing their victims as other human beings. Cases similar to Mickey's are common.

There is much disagreement about what to do to provide justice for juveniles, but most experts agree that children who show no signs of a conscience must be put in confinement for the protection of society. No one knows whether or not a different environment might have helped them to develop differently.

With the sharp rise in violent juvenile crime, there have been moves, in some areas of the country, to eliminate the juvenile court entirely. No one knows all the answers to the questions of how to handle the many different kinds of cases that become involved in the juvenile justice system. Almost all people agree that the most important approach to the juvenile crime problem is prevention.

CHAPTER FIVE

ABUSED, NEGLECTED, THROWN AWAY

Even among the thousands of children who grow up in areas where gunshots and drug dealing are more common than books and toys, there are large numbers of children who search for and find a good and meaningful way of life. Some have been in juvenile court; most of them have not. No one knows all the reasons why some young people become delinquent and others, who seem to be exposed to the same risks, do not.

Many of the cases that are heard in juvenile and family courts deal with the problems of children who have been physically, emotionally and/or sexually abused, neglected, or thrown away (put out of their homes because their families do not want them). These kinds of child abuse may not cause delinquency directly, but research sponsored by the National Institute of Justice found that childhood abuse increased the odds of future delinquency and adult criminality overall by 40 percent. Being abused, or neglected, as a child increased the likelihood of arrest as a juvenile by 55 percent, as an adult by 38 percent, and for a violent crime by 38 percent.

Poor nutrition, lack of security, and numerous other factors prevent a healthy development in those who are abused. Even those children, who are never physically abused, may suffer from the thoughtless, cruel words and harsh treatment that make them feel unworthy. One extreme example of abuse is the case of a child who was kept in a doghouse for long periods of time by his parents. His muscles could not develop properly, nor could his sense of self-esteem. One can hardly imagine how he felt. Most dogs receive more love and care.

Many abused children are taken from their parents and placed in a series of foster homes, where they must adjust to many new situations and cannot set down roots. Just being separated from their own parents is difficult, and many children carry false guilt feelings about their parents' problems.

The foster care system is so overburdened by lack of good homes and enough social workers to follow the placements, some children are forgotten by the people who are supposed to help them. Consider the case of one girl, who was sexually abused by her father. He was not permitted to visit her, but her mother asked the welfare department to place the child in a foster home because she feared that the father would return. After the girl left, the mother nailed all the windows of her house shut, carried a gun, and was eventually placed in a mental hospital. Now, the child was in limbo. She could not be adopted because there was no one to sign the release that would make her eligible for the many couples who were searching desperately for a little girl. She grew up in a series of foster homes, with no meaningful attachment. Her bad behavior and trouble with the law might have been prevented if she could have been released for adoption.

Juvenile courts have little time to deal with the problems of abused, neglected, and thrown-away kids. Important decisions that affect their whole lives must often be made without much background information. Each year about 400,000 children are forced into court through no fault of their own. During the 1980s, the number of child abuse reports grew by 176 percent, while funding for children's services was cut by $90 billion.

Judge David Soukup, a former juvenile court judge in Seattle, Washington, heard many cases in which he was asked to make decisions that seriously affected children without knowing what really had happened in their young lives. Should he return children to their homes or should he place the children in foster homes so that they would be safe from abusive parents? Would a child be less likely to become delinquent if allowed to stay with his or her natural parents? What were the details of this particular case? There was no voice for the children and no one to follow each child after placement. Social workers had too many cases to provide the necessary information that could be a thorough description of what was happening.

Back in 1976, Judge Soukup conceived the idea of asking responsible adults to speak for the children. He asked his bailiff to call four or five people who were involved with agencies that served kids in the Seattle area, and find out if they would be willing to speak for abused and neglected kids in juvenile court. The people who were contacted asked friends to join them and Judge Soukup was surprised to find fifty people at the first meeting for court-appointed guardians. These adults and those who followed them became part of an organization called CASA (Court Appointed Special Advocate Association) which was established nationally in 1982.

CASA now has 351 programs in fifty states. Approximately 30,000 volunteers speak up for abused, neglected, abandoned, and delinquent children in courts throughout the country. They help approximately 25 percent of the nation's abused and neglected children in dependency proceedings. An increasing number of CASA workers are involved in custody and delinquency cases. Volunteers come from all walks of life and vary greatly in age. But these caring people can save kids in trouble from terrible futures. CASA has been called one of the most effective changes in the juvenile justice system in the last twenty years.

Unfortunately, there are not enough CASA workers to help all the children who need them. Nor are there enough foster homes to place those who are not safe in their home. Many of the older abused and neglected children run away from their own homes and from foster homes in which they have been placed. Many people have not heard about CASA. You can help spread the word by writing a letter to your local paper, asking your parent-teacher association to have a speaker on the subject, or talking to parents and friends about this program. CASA can be reached at 206-328-8588.

Many boys and girls who find themselves in trouble with the law have been left alone by their families day after day. Consider the daily routine of a fourteen-year-old whose mother is a prostitute and whose father is in jail. He sets his alarm, gets his own breakfast, when there is food in the house, and leaves for school. After he comes home to the empty house, he invites friends to join him in smoking pot or drinking beer. If he feels tired in the morning, he doesn't bother going to school. Now and then, he borrows his mother's car, even though he has been arrested three times for driving without a license. He is one of thousands of boys and girls who spend their days without supervision. They have no reason to run away from home, for they know things would be worse on the street.

Most runaways, today, are boys and girls who are thrown out of their own home by parents who do not want them interfering with new or old relationships, especially when they are teens who are not related to the current lovers of a parent. Sometimes there is not enough money to feed and clothe boys and girls, and parents feel they can manage on their own. In many cases, the parents are addicted to drugs and find the need for the drugs more important than their children.

Kids who leave home to escape abuse, and those whose parents turn them out to live on the streets, frequently turn to juvenile prostitution. No one knows how many juvenile prostitutes there are, but estimates from law enforcement officials, social service providers, and researchers have ranged from tens of thousands to 2.4 million children annually. According to the National Runaway Switchboard in Chicago, one in three runaways is lured into prostitution within forty-eight hours of leaving home.

Many young prostitutes try to avoid police and social workers. However, others would like help but are afraid to ask for it, for fear of violent treatment from pimps. Pimps appear to be their friends early in the relationship. They may continue to supply them with some of their needs, both physical and emotional, but take a large portion of the money they make on the streets. They also threaten the kids they handle with torture, or death, if they try to leave the arrangement that has been made. Since pimps are known to follow through on their threats, it is not surprising that social workers and volunteers are viewed with apprehension when they offer shelter to boys and girls. Some kids are afraid to give up prostitution, but many would welcome a change in the life-style they were forced into because they were hungry and had no place to go.

Runaway hotlines, such as the National Runaway Switchboard (1-800-621-4000) help their callers to find runaway shelters, to return home when that is a good solution, and to get counseling. Kids in flight from troubled homes can often find a shelter that will care for them for a limited period of time. Some programs accommodate small groups; others are large. Each one tries to provide a loving, caring atmosphere with counseling in a supportive environment. Unfortunately, there are never enough runaway shelters to house all who want to live in them.

About 1.3 million teenagers live on the streets in the United States today, according to the National Runaway Switchboard. Most of them stay within 300 miles of home, but as time passes, many are drawn to urban areas. There they typically live in abandoned buildings, under bridges, and on beaches in warm climates. They live in cars, church basements, condemned apartments, the woods, and a long list of places. They scrounge for food and clothing, but they are constantly exposed to serious problems, such as violence, lack of health care and education, sexual exploitation, and fear of the law.

Many runaways find a place to live in shelters for the homeless, but these places are usually overcrowded. In some areas, there are four people who need beds for every one that is available. Even though some shelters are open to people of all ages, they are occupied almost entirely by kids. These are not kids seeking adventure, but kids who need places to live away from the abuse they knew at home, or because they are not wanted at home.

Some of the men and women in charge of shelters are frustrated because they cannot send many of the kids back to their families. The easier cases are decreasing, but there are more young people in trouble today. Even those who have not been arrested are at risk of delinquency because they have no place to go. They are too young to rent an apartment, even when a number of them pool their earnings to try to rent one. Many of them are school dropouts, who cannot find jobs, and need money to live. They get into trouble by dealing drugs or stealing in order to survive.

Blaike is a typical runaway, who says that the hardest thing about being away from home is not having any money for food, clothing, and fun. She carries a knife when she goes out in order to protect herself. Blaike is afraid of pimps, although she admits she has earned some money by offering sex to men who look for prostitutes on the street. She is afraid of these men, too, since one of them beat her and took all her money. Her friends tell her a pimp would protect her from this kind of treatment, although they admit that they have been beaten both by customers and by pimps.

Blaike has managed to steal some food from grocery stores, has stolen cigarettes, and taken wine from bag ladies. She eats at the local soup kitchen, and gets some food from emergency food shelves. Although she breaks the laws in many ways, Blaike does not think of herself as a delinquent just because she has to steal in order to survive. She plans to play on the sympathy of the judge if she ever gets caught and has to go to juvenile court.

Runaways find many ways of surviving, but most of them involve some kind of lawbreaking. According to one study, slightly over half of runaways had been arrested and over 40 percent had spent time in jail or juvenile hall. The longer the runaways in the study were away from home, the more likely they were to report arrest or having trouble with the law.

Although the 1974 Juvenile Justice and Delinquency Prevention Act encourages states to prohibit the incarceration of juveniles who are neglected, abused, in conflict with parents, runaways, and school truants in secure facilities such as training and detention centers, many of these kids find themselves in trouble with the law. One recent report from the Office of Juvenile Justice and Delinquency Prevention indicates that one in five runaway youths who were brought to the attention of authorities were admitted to secure facilities while their cases were being processed by the court.

Hundreds of thousands of children are being starved, abandoned, beaten, sexually exploited, and seriously mistreated in other ways each year. These are kids in trouble, and large numbers of them become kids in trouble with the law because of the ways they seek to solve their problems.

Kids In and Out of Trouble

Some of the ways both young people and adults can help to prevent abuse and the kids who suffer from it are suggested in the last chapter of this book and in the list of resources entitled "For Help and for More Information."

CHAPTER SIX

GROWING UP WITH GUNS AND GANGS

Kids who live in neighborhoods where there are abandoned buildings, streets and apartments full of drugs,
rats, roaches, and violence are kids at high risk for
delinquency. Many of them live in apartments that are so
crowded there is little or no privacy. Imagine trying to do
homework if you share your bedroom with four or five
brothers and sisters. You live in a building where the
elevators always smell of urine and the halls are littered
with trash. Graffiti fills the walls, and you feel unsafe
whenever you leave your apartment. You carry a knife to
protect yourself, and if someone jumps you and you stab
him, you may be the accused and be classed as the
delinquent.

About half of the fourteen-year-olds in New York City

have guns, either for protection, or for use in getting new sneakers, drugs, or whatever they want. Gun control continues to divide the nation, while state legislatures debate, and, in some cases, pass new laws that attempt to prevent the easy access to guns. The Brady Bill, which was passed late in 1993, requires that handgun purchasers be checked for records of criminality or mental instability. The law imposes a waiting period of five business days between purchase and pickup of a handgun. While this may decrease the number of guns that are sold, people in favor of gun control feel that this is only a beginning.

People who oppose gun control say, "Guns don't kill people, people kill people." Those who support gun control respond, "People try to kill people and guns kill people best." In the 1990s, support for tightening the control on the sale of many kinds of guns appeared to be growing. But teens say that they have no problem buying a gun if they want one. Many of them do.

Murders are so common in many cities that a single killing does not make headlines. There are young children, under school age, who live in inner cities and are called the 724's, because they are kept indoors seven days a week, twenty-four hours a day, so that they will not be the victims of violence. This may seem like abuse, but their parents feel it is safer than exposing them to the violence outside.

Emergency rooms in some of the local hospitals have coloring books on gun safety. One student remarked, "They kill each other as if life means nothing." New levels of violence are spreading throughout the country, as gangs and drugs reach into once peaceful plains and pastures.

In schools in the poorest sections of some cities, shootings, stabbings, and other kinds of violence are a part of life. According to a recent University of Michigan study, 19 percent of all eighth graders in the United States have been threatened by a weapon in school. This rate is much higher in some neighborhoods than others.

In many inner city schools, students feel that no one can protect them, so they have to protect themselves. They carry guns, or knives, because some of their friends have been shot. Some of the girls carry razors, hoping they will never have to use them. The National School Safety Center, a division of the United States Department of Justice, reports that there are more than three million incidents of assault, rape, robbery, and theft in America's public schools each year.

Serious incidents can arise over minor irritations, such as the wrong looks, arguments over kids bumping each other in the hall, over two boys interested in the same girl, or over someone stepping on another's foot. Suppose you go to a school where your classmates make fun of you if you do not defend yourself after someone steps on your foot. You don't want to start a fight, but kids around you insist you do something about it. They push you to the limit, and maybe you break and strike out. Or maybe you decide to let it go, even if you know you will be called a herb (a person easily intimidated).

Security measures help to protect kids inside schools in

some communities, but if someone has a "beef" (an argument or a feud) in high-risk areas, it is often settled with weapons in spite of them. Suppose a kid wants to get even with another kid, but he does not want to carry his knife past the weapon detectors at the door of the school. He just settles the beef outside the school at a place nearby where he has hidden his knife.

Metal detectors might keep homicide out of the halls, but it will take more than that to keep it out of the heart. Many criminologists emphasize the fact that there is a strong relationship between fighting crime and the social problems that contribute to it. Increased security in schools has been described as a Band-Aid approach to a problem that has deep roots in communities where poverty, drugs, and crime are widespread.

Some of the students, who are trying to get an education amidst the turmoil, welcome metal detectors and security guards, although they say having to get a pass to go to the bathroom and being searched before entering the building makes them feel like common criminals.

In spite of all the violence, in spite of the lack of caring about the law, some kids manage to stay out of trouble and make their way to a better life. Many of the kids, even in the worst schools, hope to go to college. Not everyone is "going the bad way." Most are working hard to survive in order to have a better life. They manage to stay out of trouble and to work toward careers, especially in law, medicine, social work, and sports.

The earlier kids become delinquents, the more likely

they are to continue to be offenders as adults. Many teenagers mature out of their delinquent ways before they tangle with the law. Serious injuries, counseling, the death of a friend are just some of the incidents that change the lives of kids who are at high risk for growing up to be adult criminals. Sometimes, it is an incident that scares them into realizing that there must be something better than street life.

Harry Rivera told how he changed his life in an interview for *The Christian Science Monitor*. Harry was earning hundreds of dollars selling drugs, but he was also watching other kids' lives end in violence. After he was stabbed three times by a rusty knife and he was sure he was going to die, he decided he wanted to stay alive to see his own kid grow up. With the help of counseling from social workers and support from his pregnant girlfriend, he gave up selling drugs and made plans for a different kind of future. Since the stabbing incident, he has graduated from high school and plans to train to become a paramedic. When questioned about his reasons for wanting to become a father at such an early age, Harry told his counselor that many people say it is great to have a baby now. You don't know how long you are going to live.

Feeling that they will not make it to adulthood is a reason many kids give for joining posses and gangs which, they believe, give them protection. Posses and gangs differ in definition in various geographic locations. They can be as small as a loose association of kids organized by projects, blocks, or subway stations, or they can be as large as the well-organized gangs that have units in cities throughout the United States. In the Los Angeles area, about 30,000 kids are thought to be members of posses or tribes, which are beginning to mimic gangs, and taggers, who are responsible for graffiti. Instead of firing weapons, taggers fire spray cans. Graffiti may last only a few days, because it is soon covered over by rivals, by city officials, or by other taggers who are looking for space.

Many hundreds of thousands, or perhaps more than a million, young people belong to thousands of different gangs that exist in the United States. No one knows exactly how many gangs or gang members there are, but, according to the National Institute of Justice, gang members commit violent crimes three times more often than delinquents who do not belong to gangs. In Los Angeles alone, there were 800 gang-related deaths in one year. Many of these were drive-by shootings.

Gangs and gang activities vary greatly. Some gangs are more violent than others, but almost all engage in illegal activities. Not all gangs are involved in serious drug dealing, and much crack dealing does not involve youth gangs. But young gang members are particularly susceptible to recruitment into adult criminal organizations that are engaged in large-scale drug trafficking. According to some experts, the gangs known as the Bloods and the Crips, that began in Los Angeles, controlled as much as 30 percent of the crack trade in the early 1990s.

Gang members, who use and deal drugs, cause serious violence with their drive-by shootings, turf battles, and killing of drug informers. However, there are some gangs that have become involved in making communities better. For example, two rival Detroit gangs joined to save their environment. With the help of a community program, Youth Enrichment Source, about 200 kids from two different gangs worked to remove graffiti from their neighborhood and replace it with murals.

Gangs attract young people who feel alienated from society, unappreciated, hopeless and powerless. The feeling of belonging is important to everyone, and juvenile gangs offer this sense of belonging, along with a sense of power. Unfortunately, some of the sense of power comes from possession of weapons, which often include a wide variety such as ice picks, bicycle chains, guns and assault rifles, clubs, and blackjacks. Members vary in their involvement, with some fringe gang members who are loyal but not seriously involved.

Most of the gangs are xenophobic; that is, they hate and believe false things about people of other religions, ethnic backgrounds, races, and/or sexual orientation. Kids who are raised in homes where there is a large amount of prejudice are especially attracted to gangs. So are those who live in one-parent families, those who need the gang membership to feel important, who feel gangs will supply their material needs and excitement, and/or protect them. Many kids feel they have to be tough and revenge every slight in order to survive. In a gang, brothers protect each other with their lives.

Although there are gangs of all ethnic backgrounds,

many of whom are white, blacks and Hispanics account for about 87 percent of total gang membership. Asian gangs have been growing in numbers and activity in recent years. White gangs seldom make the news, but one group received much media attention, partly because of their attitude about their criminal activities. The Spur Posse, of Lakewood, California, attracted media attention when a number of them were jailed after being accused of molesting and raping girls as young as ten. Boys in the group held a competition to see who could have sex with the largest number of girls. They were proud of their scores, even after being jailed. Although the boys claimed that the girls were willing participants, not all of the girls agreed. Some members of the Spur Posse have been indicted on other criminal offenses, but they are famous for their sexual exploits. In this case, it was not going to jail that made them heroes with their classmates as much as their sexual exploits.

Most gang members are boys, but many gangs have girls attached to them. For example, The Kings, one of San Antonio's largest gangs, accepts young women. In general, girls in the gang carry out the directives of male gang members and are considered property of the boys, but there are some gangs that have only female members. Some girl gangs have initiation for new members, while others expect most new members just to prove they can be trusted, perhaps through fighting or "ripping off" something.

Growing Up with Guns and Gangs

Picture an initiation into a girl-only gang. The girls are gathered in a part of a courtyard that is somewhat private because of construction equipment that is parked around it. After removing their heavy jewelry, they count off the seconds before the new girl's initiation begins. At that point, she is slapped and punched by the old members for a ten-second period that is counted out loud by all of them. Then the girls put back their jewelry, take out their mirrors and rearrange their hair, put on more bright red lipstick and red headbands that are part of their colors, and smooth out their black sweat suits. The new girl wipes her bloody nose, but she does not mind. She has been given a new nickname, and a sense of identity she did not have before. As soon as the girls collect dues, to be used in buying guns, they spend an evening at the home of one of the gang. They have privacy there. The girl's mother is at work and her father is in jail for incest. The new girl proudly puts on her T-shirt with the gang's colors on it.

Some females, in and out of gangs, are as ruthless as the all-male gangs. They shoot, stab, and sell drugs. Some girls help with whirlpooling, a "game" in which vulnerable girls in a swimming pool are surrounded and molested. Many girls carry guns in their pockets and razor blades in their mouths.

Various parts of the country have outlawed the wearing of colors that might be interpreted as affiliation with a gang. In addition to having to dress for safety to avoid possible symbols like those of gangs, dress codes are enforced in Detroit public schools to avoid fighting over jewelry, sneakers, and other kinds of clothing.

At least one school in New York City maintains a burial fund as part of its youth program, to help families pay to inter their children. There is a grieving room, for students to work out their sadness at the death of classmates.

Many kids who join gangs proudly wear their colors, use and sell drugs with their gangs for many years, and then come to realize that life means something else to them. They see their friends being maimed and killed or stuck in a world of getting high on drugs and suffering the lows that follow. They want to get out of the gangs, and some of them do.

Although young people in poverty neighborhoods have little to look forward to, some of them manage to find jobs, have families of their own, and visit the old gang less frequently or not at all. Gang members, who have been seriously involved in drugs and who have been in prison, are more likely to hang with the gang into adult years.

Gangs change from time to time and from place to place and from one ethnic group to another. What is true about one gang today may not be true about it tomorrow. Researchers note that even some gang members themselves may be unaware of new developments in their gang. Relatively few people study gangs on the streets in their natural setting, but much research has been done on gangs, with information obtained from gang members in prison.

Growing Up with Guns and Gangs

Gangs are being studied from many approaches, for the growth in gang-related violence now threatens the quality of life not only in housing developments but in every major city in the United States. Many rural and small city gangs identify with those in the larger cities, such as the Bloods, Crips, Vice Lords, and Folk Nation, the Los Angeles and Chicago gangs with which they are loosely connected. The gang culture reaches out to an increasing number of kids throughout the United States. Well-organized gangs introduced a variety of drugs, including crack, smokable cocaine sold as "rocks," to huge numbers of people in cities from coast to coast, and spread violent crime with it.

Even some gang leaders are saying, "The killing must stop." Participants in the National Urban Peace and Justice Summit that was held in Kansas City, Missouri, on the weekend of May 1–2, 1993, were rival gang leaders. They said that the gangs were not going to go away, but now they have to stand for positive things. These leaders hoped that they could expand this truce and that their meeting could be a springboard for a national coalition.

Gang members are facing a tough chore in their fight for new respect and a clean image. The gang problem is so complex that many people were skeptical about how much effect such meetings have in decreasing violence, but they agree that it is a step in the right direction. Truce movements have had some effect in cities such as Philadelphia, Boston, Chicago, Minneapolis, and Los Angeles, but the problems are far from over.

Kids In and Out of Trouble

Even in places where violence and despair are common, there are many kids who do not get in trouble. They say they are the invisible kids, because they do not make the headlines of the newspapers or the news programs on television. They are not the subject of movies which depict violence in the streets, but they are a very important part of society. They are the hope of tomorrow.

CHAPTER SEVEN

IN TROUBLE WITH DRUGS

G angs and guns were not the cause of all the violence that surged in the past decade, but they made it more deadly. According to the National Council on Crime and Delinquency, a large proportion of crimes are committed by drug users. Many teens use drugs, and not all of them are abusers. But drugs and violence are connected in a number of ways, and many users and dealers find themselves in trouble with the law.

Kids use alcohol and other drugs for many reasons. Among them are: to feel good, for fun, to rebel, to please peers, because the media makes tobacco and alcohol appear glamorous, to avoid stress, and to escape painful situations. Many adults, who do the same, tend to look down on kids who use drugs even though they do not consider themselves as drug users and abusers. This is especially true for adults who abuse alcohol and tobacco, drugs that are legal for them.

After years of declining drug use among high school students, a report issued in 1993 by University of Michigan researchers indicated that there was a trend toward more drug use by the youngest teens. Marijuana, cocaine, LSD, and other hallucinogen use was much greater than in the previous year. Dr. Lloyd Johnson, chief investigator in the study at Michigan, suggests that the younger teens have not heard as much about the dangers of drugs as older teens. For example, almost all kids know that injecting heroin is bad, but many think it is safe to sniff and smoke the drug, even though it can actually be just as bad.

In the summer of 1993, the Department of Health and Human Services reported a record number of drug-related visits to emergency rooms in one recent month. The number of emergency room visits is an indicator of the amount of hard-core drug use. In July of 1993, Dr. Johnson and other researchers at the University of Michigan reported that the use of marijuana and LSD was gaining on college campuses after a period of decline.

Although the use of cocaine has been affected by increased awareness of the damage it can cause, this is not true for many other drugs. No one questions the fact that many of today's kids are in trouble with drugs.

Malt liquor, which has a higher alcohol content than regular beer, became very popular in the early '90s. One brand has more alcohol in the popular 40-ounce bottle than a six-pack of beer. Some teenagers drank a bottle on the way to school, getting a cheap high and a good start on becoming an alcoholic. At "hooky parties" in basements and on rooftops, 40-ounce bottles of malt liquor, commonly known as 40's, earned the nickname "liquid crack" because, like crack, it was a way to get a cheap high.

Patterns of drug abuse change from year to year. Among people of all ages, the overall use of illegal drugs appears to be down, but heavy and high-risk use of the most disabling drugs may be greater than ever. Emergency room visits by drug abusers began to increase in number in 1991, and by 1993, they had set a new record.

Crack, the smokable and inexpensive cocaine, came to Los Angeles in 1980, and by 1983, crack houses, where people gather to use crack, appeared in certain Los Angeles neighborhoods. In the following decade, crack use spread throughout many cities in the United States. By 1990, the National Cocaine Hotline estimated that over a million Americans had tried this form of cocaine.

The crack epidemic struck with great force, partly because crack was cheap and easily available, and partly because the conditions were ripe as social programs were cut.

With the increase in cocaine use came an increase in violence. The murder rate in Washington, D.C. increased by 151 percent after the introduction of crack, the cheap form of cocaine that is so addictive that users do just about anything to get the next fix. Users have been known to sell their own furniture, jewelry, clothing, and cars, and to have broken into their own parents' homes to steal their money, electronic equipment, and anything that they can sell to get more money for crack. One woman is reported to have sold her baby's crib; another to have earned drug money by allowing men to rape her daughter. Crack makes some people more paranoid (fearful of things that do not exist) and more violent than most other drugs.

PCP (phencyclidine), also known as angel dust, continues to be popular in spite of the many tragedies that have been reported by emergency room and other health workers. In the case of Cheryl, a quiet girl who planned a career in journalism, PCP changed her life. She fell in love with a boy who sold PCP and he introduced her to it. Although she had several wonderful experiences after using it, one time she became very aggressive. She argued with an amusement park security officer about removing her rag, the bandanna that dangled from her pocket to show her loyalty to her gang. When he tried to take it, she stabbed him in the stomach with the knife she carried for her own protection. She was arrested and sentenced to eighteen months in jail, during which time she experienced some unpleasant backflashes. But she went back to school after she was released on probation. Part of her probation included community service in a drug treatment program, and Cheryl feels that this is one of the most rewarding parts of her life. She plans to be a social worker. Cheryl still has tattoos on her arms that show her loyalty to her lover's gang, but she is going through a series of treatments to have them removed.

In Trouble with Drugs

Trish had a very different experience. She grew up in a suburban area, where many kids experimented with drugs. Alcohol was the drug of choice for most of her friends. They partied and drank to get drunk every Saturday night, but few of them were arrested. Several had their licenses revoked for drunk driving, and one boy was so drunk that he fell out of the window at a fraternity house and was seriously injured. Most of her group grew out of their binge drinking and became social drinkers, people who stop drinking before they are drunk. About 10 percent became alcoholics, who had no control over their drinking. This happens among rich and poor, among almost all ethnic cultures, and in all parts of the United States. No one knows all the answers to why some people become alcoholics and others do not, but heredity appears to play a part.

Jessica's father is a lawyer and her mother is a doctor. They expect her to get all A's on every report card, and she tries very hard to please them. Some of her friends drink at their parties, but Jessica has been warned that she should not start to drink. She has heard stories about many of her relatives who became alcoholics, and her mother told her she might be at risk. One afternoon, after a bad report on her schoolwork, Jessica went with her friends to the local hangout. They had a case of beer, and Jessica, who decided to drown her sorrows, took her first drink. She felt great, and she continued to drink until she was so drunk that her friends took her to a park where she slept until she was sober.

Kids In and Out of Trouble

Jessica promised herself that she would never drink again, but she continued to do so, getting drunk each time. One night she insisted on driving home from a party, and she had an accident. At this point, Jessica's parents became aware of her problem and they helped her to enter a treatment program. She was in trouble with the law, but she was put on probation because her parents promised to help her. For most poor children, this is not an alternative.

About 17 million people in the United States are estimated to be suffering from an alcohol problem in any given year, according to the National Council on Alcoholism and Drug Dependency. Alcohol abuse is related to many physical problems, such as liver disease and poor nutrition. Overall, the 100,000 deaths in America attributed to alcohol each year are some twenty times those attributed to illegal drugs. Nicotine in cigarettes, chewing tobacco, pipes, cigars, and snuff is responsible for about four times as many deaths as alcohol. Lung cancer, heart disease, mouth cancer, and strokes are just a few of the health problems related to tobacco, which accounts for about one in five premature deaths in the United States each year. Both tobacco and alcohol are illegal for young people, but not for adults. Both are potential causes of death in the long run.

Although many young people use a wide variety of drugs illegally, no one knows which kids will get in trouble because they will become addicted or will get in trouble with the law. The following case illustrates this.

Carlos does not want to deal drugs, but he is desperate to be popular, cannot find a job, and his parents are sick. He needs money to help them and drug dealing looks more inviting than staying in school. He wonders if he will live long enough to get a regular job.

In some gangs and in many families at all social levels, an addict is considered a fiend. Although there is considerable drug use among gang members, the heavy user is not admired. Nor is he or she considered acceptable in other parts of society.

One of the drugs that is being used more at all levels is LSD (lysergic acid diethylamide). Since today's LSD is usually less potent than that used by the flower children of the 1960s, there is a general belief that it is safe. But this drug, and other hallucinogens (drugs that produce unreal sensations, such as seeing visions and hearing voices) produce many bad reactions. Hospitals reported a 65 percent increase in LSD-related emergency room admissions between 1985 and 1990. About half of these patients were under the age of twenty.

Heroin, a drug that has been used for a very long time, is another drug that is increasing in popularity. Heroin has always played a part in crime, but for reasons different from the violence that came with crack. Heroin users are known for their sleepy highs and the addiction that leads to crime when they steal for more drug money. Heroin addicts need increased amounts of drug in order to get high, or even feel normal. A habit can cost hundreds of dollars a day, and is financed by selling drugs, stealing, or both.

Eric started smoking pot in his first year of high school, when he joined a band that let him play his beloved bass fiddle. He liked the nice, woozy high that pot gave him and the way it made the lights and colors look. He only smoked on weekends, and he managed to stay in school. But he hated school and he loved the band and the friends he made in the group. One of these friends kept telling Eric how much he was missing by not using horse (heroin). One night when he was high on pot, he decided it would not hurt just to try it once. "I'm not going to get hooked," he said with disdain. "I'm not going to become a junkie." Eric and his friend snorted some heroin together. At first, Eric felt sick in his stomach, but the nausea passed and then he got extremely high.

In the next few months, Eric left his old friends, quit school, and hung around with the band from the time he got up until the time he went to bed. He found the whole scene exciting. He had numerous girls and the wonderful night life he had dreamed about. Each night, he and his new friends snorted heroin. Although he now was snorting on a daily basis, Eric was sure *he* was not an addict. He knew that people who snort heroin look down on people who shoot it. Eric figured it was the people who used the needle who were crazy. They were the ones who had a problem, not him.

In Trouble with Drugs

Eric traveled with his small band to a city about a hundred miles from home. One morning he woke up without any money to buy his heroin. He was having chills, and he felt really sick. He went for a walk, wearing his overcoat, even though it was hot outside. A junkie he knew walked up to him, saw that he was sweating and took him to a heroin shooting gallery. He gave Eric a shot of heroin, and he was high almost immediately. The runny nose, the cramps, and the sweating stopped, and he felt good again. Eric had always been afraid of using a needle, but he got over that fear fast. He also had to accept the fact that he was a real junkie.

Eric thought about seeking treatment, but there were not enough places in any of the programs to which he applied. Many heroin users, who would like to stop, experience the same problem. Waiting lists are long in spite of the fact that studies show that the most effective way to curb drug abuse lies in prevention and treatment.

Getting involved with drugs is easy. Suppose your twelve-year-old brother is the only one in the neighborhood without $200 sneakers. His life at home is grim. Food is scarce. Your father left long ago and your mother tries to keep the family together with her job at the hospital. Her hours are long and your brother is left alone much of the time. He has learned about right and wrong and he is a good kid. But when he goes out on the street, he is the only one wearing cheap sneakers. The other kids pressure him into selling crack so he can buy $200 sneakers like theirs. He knows he may get into trouble someday if he sells crack, but he is twelve years old. Someday may never happen. If it does, it is probably far away.

Drugs can be found in just about every community and in every school. Cocaine and heroin are cheaper and more freely available than in the past, and almost everyone knows where to find kids who are glad to sell drugs.

Through drug prevention programs, both in neighborhoods and schools, many young kids have decided not to start. They are helping to clean up the parks, the street corners, and teaching their younger brothers and sisters to stay away from drugs. Knowing about the negative effects that drugs have had on many older teens has played a large part in helping to keep kids from starting. They believe the slogan, BE SMART, DON'T START.

But what about those who *have* started? The Federal government has spent millions of dollars trying to close the borders of the United States to prevent drugs from entering, but drugs continue to arrive by plane, boat, and truck, and in almost unimaginable ways. In addition to the so-called illegal drugs, there is easy access to alcohol and tobacco, drugs that are illegal for kids.

Arresting drug users has increased since the introduction of the Federal Anti-Drug Abuse Act of 1986, requiring prison sentences for anyone carrying small amounts of drugs, as well as for major dealers. As a result, prisons are full, courts are overwhelmed with drug cases, and many of the big dealers are free to continue business as usual.

New calls for greater access to treatment are helping some kids who get in trouble with the law. But in 1994, there were only enough drug treatment centers to handle one-third of the estimated six million heavy drug abusers. Not all of them want treatment, but there are many more who want it than receive it.

According to John C. Higgins-Biddle, executive director of the Connecticut Alcohol and Drug Abuse Commission, the government's approach of jailing drug users has overburdened the court and prison system, but it has done little to halt the destruction that drug abuse has inflicted on communities. Is this true in your state?

No one can solve the plague of drug addiction, but education and additional treatment centers can decrease the number of kids in trouble because of drug use and abuse.

CHAPTER EIGHT

KIDS CAN MAKE A DIFFERENCE

What can kids do to help other kids in trouble? Some can do a little; some can do a lot. Activities range from tutoring a classmate to saving lives in an ambulance corps, from learning nonviolent ways to settle differences to serving on an advisory council of youths who make young people accountable for their actions.

Youth service organizations around the country report a surge of interest among young people in helping to take charge of what is happening in their world. A report called "Volunteering and Giving Among American Teenagers, 12 to 17 Years of Age" indicates that 61 percent of American teens average 3.2 hours of volunteer activity per week. In one year, teens contributed 2.1 billion hours of activity.

Kids Can Make a Difference

Young people have been called the hope for a less violent society and a vital resource in meeting pressing needs in communities throughout the nation. They make a difference in many different ways. For example, kids known as Youth Force began a program in New York City called "Take Back the Park" in which the original staff organizers range in age from fifteen to nineteen and were considered "high risk" for getting into trouble. They invited young people and a few community leaders to join them in their planning and action. Through fliers and posters, they gathered the support of well over a thousand kids, who joined them having fun in the park with music, films, crafts, workshops, and youth speakout. Many who had been hanging out on the street took part in programs that were fun. They joined in protesting drugs and prostitution, and they made a difference in their neighborhood.

For some inner-city kids, the danger of violence is so great that they cannot safely organize on the streets and in the parks, but many are helped by community service organizations. For example, in New York City, The CityKids Foundation has an active membership of 3,000 and programming that involves more than 50,000 young people each year. Members produce programs that focus on self-esteem, education, environmental awareness, AIDS, drugs, crime, health and global issues. Some members perform in schools and communities, teach others how to be leaders, volunteer in homeless hotels and communities, produce television programs, plan special events, conduct creative literary workshops, and more. CityKids programs reach many people across the United States. At least one program, excerpts from "CityKids Speak on Growing Up and Other Heroic Deeds," is estimated to have had a worldwide television audience of 10 million people.

Another organization, Youth Service America, with headquarters in Washington, D.C., sustains a national network of quality service programs. These provide people of all ages and backgrounds with opportunities in leadership that help young people begin a lifelong commitment to community improvement and participation. Youth Service America is the principal sponsor of an annual National Youth Service Day, recognizing the service of nearly one million young people nationwide.

The Kids Guide to Social Action: How to Solve the Social Problems You Choose—and Turn Creative Thinking into Positive Action by Barbara Lewis suggests many ways in which you can make a difference. Your librarian may be able to help you obtain this book.

Thousands of young people have joined groups such as Student Crime Stoppers, who report crime without fear of reprisal through hotlines. Student Crime Stopper programs have made a difference in schools that range from elementary level to college. In addition to supplying tips for police and school security, these programs are providing a new awareness and changing many attitudes about crime and community involvement. Student Crime Stopper programs are part of Crime Stoppers International, that publishes a guide on how to begin a unit in your school with the help of your principal and a support network. For more information, call 1-800-245-0009.

Programs like Teens on Target in Oakland, California, help to spread the word about the dangers of gun violence. They emphasize that getting shot does not always mean that you die, as it seems to do so often on television. Rather than dying in glory, the victim may spend the rest of his life in a wheelchair. They point out that anesthesia does not always take effect before the emergency room physician starts probing for the bullet. In similar programs, teens alert each other to the real risks of gun violence, how to resist peer pressure, and how to tell the difference between what happens on television and on the street.

Many young people have shown that they can make a difference through programs such as SADD, Students Against Driving Drunk. SADD, which was founded in 1981 by Robert Anastas, has grown so that it is now international. There are over 25,000 SADD chapters in middle schools, high schools, and colleges in the United States with over 5 million members. Members sign a contract with parents in which members agree to call for advice and/or transportation at any hour, any place, if they are ever in a situation where they have been drinking, or someone who would be driving them has been drinking. Parents agree to provide the transportation and to discuss it at a later time. SADD is credited with helping to lower the American teen alcohol crash death rate by more than two-thirds.

Kids In and Out of Trouble

Teens have shown that they are willing to take a stand against drunk driving for themselves and for their friends. When SADD began, many people said that young people were not responsible, would not be willing to resist peer pressure, and would not make such a program work. They have been proven wrong.

Now SADD is targeting alcohol abuse and addiction, since drinking is a factor in at least half of the accidents that result from drowning, falls, gun incidents, boat and snowmobile crashes. The risk of teen pregnancy, violence, sexually transmitted diseases, and dropping out of school increase when kids use alcohol or other drugs. According to SADD, teens develop alcoholism and other addiction problems more quickly than adults.

Many programs led by peers are showing remarkable success in helping kids in trouble, as well as preventing them from breaking the law. Peer tutoring and counseling programs are especially successful, whether education-oriented or health-oriented. Peer leaders, who are slightly older than the teens they help, do well in teaching social skills that help kids resist pressures to use drugs or enter into unprotected sex. They also help to identify and practice healthful activities for younger kids.

One of the most outstanding programs in which older teens help younger new volunteers has been the Emergency Medical Service in Darien, Connecticut. This ambulance service has been staffed by boys and girls between the ages of fourteen to eighteen since 1969.

Imagine regaining consciousness after an automobile

accident to find that a teenager is administering oxygen to you, checking your pulse, and feeling your arm for a possible fracture. The only people in sight, other than firemen and police, are teens. They have secured your body to a backboard, and they are sliding you into an ambulance. Even the driver is a teen. All of these people have been trained to handle emergencies and to do so well.

About thirty boys and thirty girls, under the direction of an adult supervisor, run the emergency rescue team twenty-four hours a day. Members are known as Posties, because the emergency service was organized by the Boy Scout Explorer Post 53. Teens on duty wear pagers that go off in an emergency when they are at school, playing sports, at home, or wherever they might be. The crew responds immediately to the 911 calls relayed from the police to the teen on duty in the radio room and to them. They meet the older teen driver of the ambulance at the scene of the emergency, for drivers keep the ambulance with them at school, at home, or wherever they might be. The group springs into action, working with the proficiency that has won the organization many awards. The local hospital director of emergency service says, "They're as good as any professional operation in the state."

Each emergency is different, and they cope with many kinds. These teens deliver babies, administer CPR, and make many life and death decisions. A young adult is trained to do advanced life support, diagnosis, and shock control, but the younger teens are trained and certified in the Basic Life Support Level and Emergency Medical Techniques. Each member goes through 300 hours of training and repeated testing of knowledge and technical expertise. Membership in the Emergency Medical System is highly competitive, and it is not for everyone. A great deal of dedication is needed.

The kids of this and many other members of life-saving 911 emergency rescue teams are unusual volunteers. Not many young people have the opportunity to help in such exciting ways, but it is important for everyone to work toward the goal of making things better.

Kids in Vermont have been lobbying their state legislature for several years. Beginning with a candlelight vigil for children's rights to basic needs such as pure drinking water, shelter, basic education, and protection from violence, the movement has grown under the leadership of Neva Pratico, a third-grade teacher in Clarendon, Vermont. Governor Howard Dean of Vermont proclaimed an annual Rights of the Child Day as a result of the appeals of Vermont students, and Vermont Senator Patrick Leahy read a resolution that was passed into the Congressional Record.

Kids can make a difference in developing tolerance for people of different ethnic groups. Education at various age levels is playing a part. White children in some schools learn that many blacks and Hispanics want the same things they want and that they, too, fear the violence. But many white adults fear all blacks, believing that blacks attack whites more than people of their own color. This is not the case. Most of the killers and most of the victims are young black men, and many blacks and Hispanics are as upset by the inner-city violence as people of other colors are.

Homicide is the leading cause of death for black teenagers in the United States, and there is much peer pressure for blacks to have guns to defend themselves. For many of them, pride is all they have, and some feel that defending it is most important. One boy described his life as selling drugs, hanging out, and trying to stay alive. However, strong voices are being raised among the young in black communities to halt the violence in which blacks kill blacks.

If you feel hopeless about the problems of people in inner cities and about kids in trouble, imagine how they feel. No matter where you live, you can probably find some way to help others, and find rewards in doing so. Young people are participating in groups that work toward less violence in television, violence prevention programs in schools, better sex education in schools, making schools safer, working in soup kitchens, educating the disadvantaged, and many more. Urban youth corps, groups of people who are engaged in rebuilding and revitalizing poor communities, offer promise. There are more than thirty youth corps nationwide, and there is hope that they will be effective in helping at-risk youth.

By 1994, many states were adopting a requirement of community service for public high school students. Service experiences range from tree planting to lobbying the legislature, but many kinds involved kids helping kids in areas such as counseling and tutoring. Public school districts in about twenty-five states had compulsory programs requiring some volunteer work before students could graduate from high school. Many private schools also require community service. In September, 1993, Maryland became the first state to require service as a condition of graduation for all high school students. While some students feel that requiring community service programs is unconstitutional, and some treat it as a joke and do the minimum required, others find that they enjoy their work at places such as museums, hospitals, and day-care centers, and do more than they are required to do.

There is much to be done to help children who are badly warped by their environments, and there is increasing recognition that students who participate in community service programs heighten their own self-esteem and build a sense of responsibility as well as providing help for kids who are at risk of trouble with the law.

Youth Against Crime is a program organized by Connecticut Congresswoman Rosa L. DeLauro that began regular monthly meetings in twenty-six high schools in Connecticut in 1994. Students in the program involve themselves with crime issues by discussing them and vocalizing possible solutions. Committees, such as media and law enforcement groups, organize the ideas that are discussed and present them to adults who work locally in each field. Young people in this and other programs agree that their involvement in solutions to violence is important.

Kids Can Make a Difference

Youth as Resources (YAR) engages youth in services to their communities and challenges them to take responsibility for improving their communities. YAR is governed by local boards of youth and adults. More than 40,000 young volunteers, ranging in age from five through twenty-one years, have completed several thousand projects that address a wide variety of social issues.

Many young people are writing to their congressmen asking for their help in keeping kids out of trouble. Personal detailed letters on violence-related topics can carry clout. You might begin a letter with "I wish I had a safe place to play," or "I'm afraid to go to school," or other problems that exist because so many kids in your neighborhood are in trouble. Write senators at the U.S. Senate, Washington, D.C. 20510 and representatives at the U.S. House of Representatives, Washington, D.C. 20515.

While kids themselves can make some difference in helping other kids in trouble, people of all ages need to work toward making juveniles accountable for their actions and making society accountable for conditions that play a major part in leading kids to delinquency.

Awareness can be a beginning toward large-scale action. Schools, religious groups, and other local community-based organizations help children to develop into productive law-abiding citizens. Everyone can support some of the many organizations that work with children in one way or another. Some of these organizations are listed at the end of this book.

Kids In and Out of Trouble

One of the greatest challenges facing the juvenile justice system is to provide consistent services both before cases get to court and afterwards. A national priority of early intervention to keep kids out of trouble is more important in today's world than ever.

For Help and for More Information

Many organizations and government agencies supply information at low or no cost. Your phone book may help you to find local groups that are involved in helping kids in trouble. Many hotlines can provide instant help.

FOR INFORMATION:

CASA (Court Appointed Special Advocate Association)
1-206-328-8588

Drugs and Crime Data Center and Clearinghouse
1-800-666-3332

Juvenile Justice Clearinghouse
1-800-638-8736

For Help and for More Information

National Center for Missing and Exploited Children
1-703-235-3900
To report a missing child: 1-800-843-5678

National Clearinghouse for Alcohol and Drug
Information
1-800-SAY-NO-TO

National Committee for Prevention of Child Abuse
1-703-739-0321

National Council on Child Abuse and Family Violence
1-800-222-2000

National Crime Prevention Council
1-800-WE-PREVENT

National Criminal Justice Reference Service (NCJRS)
1-800-851-3420

National Institute of Justice
1-800-851-3420

National Victims Resource Center
1-800-627-6872

TOLL-FREE HOTLINES:

1-800-356-9996: Al-Anon Family Groups, Inc. provides
help for family members of alcoholics.

1-800-286-2229: Baby Your Baby provides information
and references for pregnant women.

For Help and for More Information

1-800-Cocaine: National Cocaine Hotline counselors offer guidance and refer drug users to public and private treatment centers.

1-800-NCA-CALL: National Council on Alcoholism provides referrals and state and local affiliates.

1-800-662-HELP: National Institute of Drug Abuse Referral Line directs callers to local abuse treatment centers. Free materials are available.

1-800-342-AIDS: National AIDS Hotline provides information to general public and help for people with AIDS.

1-800-621-4000: National Runaway Switchboard operators will provide confidential help.

1-800-231-6946: Runaway Hotline operators provide confidential help.

Glossary of Terms

Adjudicated: Judged to be a delinquent or status offender.

Advocate: To speak out, or write, in favor of an idea or cause.

Alienated: Made to feel unfriendly, hostile, or indifferent.

Arrest: Depriving a person of his or her liberty; taking a person into custody for the purpose of formally charging him or her with a crime.

Assault: Unlawful intentional inflicting, or attempted or threatened inflicting, of injury upon another person.

Burglary: Unlawful entry, or attempted entry, of any fixed structure, vehicle, or structure used for regular residence, industry, or business, with or without force, with intent to commit a felony or larceny.

Criminal homicide: Causing the death of another person

without legal justification or excuse. The term, in law, embraces all homicides where the perpetrator intentionally killed someone without legal justification, or accidentally killed someone as a consequence of reckless or grossly negligent conduct. It includes all conduct encompassed by the terms murder, voluntary manslaughter, involuntary manslaughter, and vehicular manslaughter.

Criminal justice system: The agencies responsible for enforcing criminal laws.

Criminologist: A person who studies crime.

Delinquency: Acts or conduct in violation of criminal law.

Delinquent act: An act committed by a juvenile for which an adult could be prosecuted in criminal court, but when it is committed by a juvenile is within the jurisdiction of the juvenile court.

Detention center: A short-term facility that provides custody in a physically restricting environment pending adjudication or, following adjudication, pending disposition, placement, or transfer.

Detention camp, ranch, or farm: A long-term residential facility for persons whose behavior does not require the strict confinement of a training school, often allowing greater contact with the community.

Dispositional hearing: Held by juvenile and family court to determine the disposition of children after cases have been adjudicated.

Felony: A serious type of offense, such as murder, armed robbery, or rape.

Gang: A somewhat organized group of some duration,

sometimes characterized by turf concerns, symbols, special dress, and colors. It has special interest in violence for status-providing purposes and is recognized as a gang both by its members and by others.

Graffiti: Drawing or writing on walls and other public places.

Group home: A long-term nonconfining facility in which residents are allowed extensive access to community resources, such as schooling, employment, health care, and cultural events.

Incest: Sexual intercourse between two persons where marriage between them is forbidden by law.

Juvenile: A person under an age (usually age eighteen) specified by state statute who is subject to juvenile authority at the time of admission.

Halfway house: See group home.

Heroin: A powerful sedative drug derived from morphine.

LSD (lysergic acid diethylamide): A powerful drug that produces hallucinations, the illusion of seeing or hearing something that is not present.

Marijuana: Dried leaves, stems, and flowering tops of the hemp plant, usually smoked in cigarette form.

Offender: A person who breaks the law.

PCP (phencylidine): Highly addictive drug that causes hallucinations, and frequently causes aggressive, uncontrollable behavior. Commonly called angel dust.

Posses: Forces of men or squads.

Rape: Sexual intercourse, or attempted sexual intercourse, with an individual against her or his will by force or threat of force.

Reception or diagnostic center: A short-term facility that screens persons committed by courts and assigns them to appropriate custody facilities.

Robbery: Unlawful taking, or attempted taking, of property that is in the immediate possession of another by force or the threat of force.

Self-esteem: A good opinion of oneself.

Shelter: A short-term facility that provides temporary care similar to that of a detention center but in a physically unrestricted environment.

Status offenses: Acts or conduct which are offenses only when committed by juveniles, and which can be adjudicated only by a juvenile court. Although state statutes defining status offenses vary, the following types of offenses are usually classified as status offenses:

Running away: Leaving the custody and home of parents, guardians, or custodians without permission and failing to return within a reasonable length of time, in violation of statutes regulating the conduct of youth.

Truancy: Violation of a compulsory school attendance law.

Ungovernability: Being beyond the control of parents, guardians, or custodians, or disobedient of parental authority, referred to in various juvenile codes as unmanageable, unruly, incorrigible, etc.

State liquor law violations: Violation of laws regulating the possession, purchase, or consumption by minors. In some states, consumption of alcohol and public drunkenness by juveniles is a status offense, in others it is classed as delinquency.

Other status offenses: Tobacco violation, curfew violation, and violation of a court order.

Training school: A long-term facility for adjudicated juvenile offenders typically under strict physical and staff controls.

Youthful offender: A person adjudicated in criminal court who may be above the statutory age limit for juveniles but below a specified upper age limit and for whom special correctional commitment and record-sealing procedures are made available by statute.

Bibliography

Baker, Falcon. *Saving Our Kids from Delinquency, Drugs and Despair*. New York: HarperCollins, 1991.

Bennet, Georgette. *Crime Warps: The Future of Crime in America*. Garden City, New York: Doubleday, 1987.

Berger, Gilda. *Addiction*. New York: Watts, 1992.

———. *Violence and Drugs*. New York: Watts, 1989.

Bing, Leon. *Do or Die*. New York: HarperCollins, 1991.

Bode, Janet. *Beating the Odds: Stories of Unexpected Achievers*. New York: Watts, 1992.

Brown, Gene. *Violence on America's Streets*. Brookfield, CT: Millbrook Press, 1992.

Brown, Waln K. *The Other Side of Delinquency*. New Brunswick, NJ: Rutgers University Press, 1983.

Bibliography

Bureau of Justice Statistics Bulletins. United States Department of Justice. "The Catalyst." Washington, D.C.: Crime Prevention Coalition. 1991 to current issues.

Chesney-Lind, Meda, and Shelden, Randall. *Girls, Delinquency and Juvenile Justice*. Florence, KY: Wadsworth, Inc., 1993.

Cohen, Alan M. *Kids Out of Control*. Washington, D.C.: Psychiatric Institute of America Press, 1989.

Currie, Elliott. *Reckoning: Drugs, the Cities and the American Future*. New York: Hill and Wang, 1993.

Dash, L. *When Children Want Children: The Urban Crisis of Teenage Childbearing*. New York: William Morrow, 1989.

DePanfilis, Diane and Salus, Marsha. *A Coordinated Response to Child Abuse and Neglect: A Basic Manual*. Washington, D.C.: National Center on Child Abuse and Neglect, 1992.

Dryfoos, J. G. *Adolescents at Risk: Prevalence and Prevention*. New York: Oxford University Press, 1990.

"Drugs and Violence: Causes, Correlates and Consequences." National Institute of Drug Abuse Monograph Series. Research Monograph 103.

Edelman, Marion Wright. *The Measure of Our Success: A Letter to My Children and Yours*. Boston: Beacon Press, 1992.

Ewing, Charles Patrick. *Kids Who Kill*. New York: Avon Books, 1992.

Falco, Matheo. *The Making of a Drug Free America: Programs That Work*. New York: Random House/Times Books, 1992.

Bibliography

Federal Register. "First Comprehensive Plan for Fiscal Year 1993." Washington, D.C.: Office of Juvenile Justice and Delinquency Prevention, 1993.

Francis, Dorothy B. *Shoplifting: The Crime Everybody Pays For.* New York: Lodestar Books, 1979.

———. *Vandalism: The Crime of Immaturity.* New York: Lodestar Books, 1983.

Gardner, Sandra. *Street Gangs in America.* New York: Watts, 1992.

Gill, Charles D. "Essay on the State of the American Child, 2000 A.D.: Chattel or Constitutionally Protected Child Citizen." Ohio Northern University: Law Review. Volume XVII, Number 3, 1991.

Greenberg, Keith Elliot. *Out of the Gang.* Minneapolis, MN: Lerner, 1992.

Greenleaf, Barbara K. *Children Through the Ages: A History of Childhood.* New York: McGraw-Hill, 1978.

Grinney, Ellen Heath. *Delinquency and Criminal Behavior.* New York: Chelsea House, 1992.

Hatkoff, Amy, and Klopp, Karen Kelly. *How to Save the Children.* New York: Fireside Books/Simon & Schuster, 1992.

Hamburg, David A. *Today's Children: Creating a Future for a Generation in Crisis.* New York: Times Books/Random House, 1992.

Hechinger, Fred M. *Fateful Choices: Healthy Youth for the 21st Century.* New York: Hill and Wang, 1993.

Hjelmeland, Andy. *Kids in Jail.* Minneapolis, MN: Lerner, 1992.

Bibliography

Hyde, Margaret O. *Know About Abuse.* New York: Walker and Company, 1992.

———. *Teen Sex.* Louisville, KY: The Westminster Press, 1988.

———. *The Violent Mind.* New York: Watts, 1992.

Janus, Mark-David, and others. *Adolescent Runaways: Causes and Consequences.* Lexington, MA: Lexington Books, 1987.

Johnson, Jean J. *Kids without Homes.* New York: Watts, 1992.

———. *Teen Prostitution.* New York: Watts, 1992.

"Juvenile Alcohol and Other Drug Abuse: A Guide to Federal Initiatives for Prevention, Treatment and Control." Office of Juvenile Justice and Delinquency Prevention, 1992.

"Juvenile Justice." Washington, D.C. Office of Juvenile Justice and Delinquency Prevention, U.S. Department of Justice. Volume 1, Number 1, Spring/Summer 1993, and following issues.

Kotlowitz, Alex. *There Are No Children Here: The Story of Two Boys Growing Up in Urban America.* New York: Doubleday, 1991.

Kramer, Rita. *At a Tender Age: Violent Youth and Juvenile Justice.* New York: Henry Holt, 1988.

Krogh, David. *Smoking: The Artificial Passion.* New York: Freeman, 1992.

Kulin, Susan G. *What Do I Know? Talking About Teenage Pregnancy.* New York: Putnam, 1991.

Lang, Susan S. *Teen Violence.* New York: Watts, 1992.

Bibliography

Lefkowitz, Bernard. *Tough Change: Growing Up on Your Own in America.* New York: The Free Press, 1987.

Lewis, Barbara. *The Kid's Guide to Social Action: How to Solve the Social Problems You Choose—and Turn Creative Thinking into Positive Action.* Minneapolis, MN: Free Spirit, 1991.

Magid, Ken, and McKelvey, Carole. *High Risk: Children Without a Conscience.* New York: Bantam Books, 1987.

Miller, Jerome G. *Last One Over the Wall: The Massachusetts Experiment in Closing Reform Schools.* Columbus, OH: Ohio State University Press, 1991.

National Commission on Children. "Beyond Rhetoric: A New American Agenda for Children and Families." Washington, D.C.: National Commission on Children, 1991.

———. "Juvenile Justice Policy Statement." Francis Terry, ed, 1991.

National Council of Juvenile and Family Court Judges. *Disposition Resource Manual.* Reno, NV: University of Nevada, 1992.

National Council on Crime and Delinquency. "Drug Policy Statement." Francis Terry, ed., 1991.

National Crime Prevention Council. Various publications.

National Institute for Citizen Education in the Law and National Crime Prevention Council. "Teens, Crime, and Community." St. Paul, MN: West Publishing Company, 1988.

Office of Juvenile Justice and Delinquency Prevention. "Juveniles Taken into Custody." Fiscal Year Reports.

Office of Substance Abuse Prevention. "Turning Awareness into Action: What Your Community Can Do About Drug Use in America." Washington, D.C.: DHHS Publication No. ADM 91-1562, 1991.

———. "What You Can Do About Drug Use in America." Washington, D.C.: DHHS Publication, ADM 91-1572, 1991.

Parks, Peggy L, and Arndt, Edward K. "Differences Between Adolescent and Adult Mothers of Infants." *Journal of Adolescent Health Care II*, 1990, pp. 248–253.

"Prevention of Mental Disorders, Alcohol, and Other Drug Use in Children and Adolescents." Rockville, MD: OSAP Prevention Monograph 2, Office of Substance Abuse Prevention, 1989.

Reiss, Albert J., and Roth, Jeffrey A. *Understanding Tomorrow*. Washington, D.C.: National Academy Press, 1993.

Rohr, Janeele, ed. *Violence in America: Opposing Viewpoints*. San Diego, CA: Greenhaven Press, 1990.

Rossman, Parker. *After Punishment What? Discipline and Reconciliation*. New York: Collins, 1980.

Sereny, Gitta. *The Invisible Children: Child Prostitution in America, West Germany, and Great Britain*. New York: Knopf, 1985.

Spergel, Irving A. *Youth Gangs: Continuity and Change in Crime and Justice*, Vol. 12. Ed. by Michael Tonry and Norval Morris. Chicago, IL: University of Chicago Press, 1990, pp. 171–275.

———. *Youth Gangs: Problems and Response*. Executive Summary. Washington, D.C.: Office of Juvenile Justice and Delinquency Prevention,1990.

Bibliography

Springer, Charles E. *Justice for Juveniles*. Washington, D.C.: United States Department of Justice, 1987.

Strahinich, Helen. *Think About Guns in America*. New York: Walker, 1992.

Temple, Todd. *How to Rearrange the World*. Washington, D.C., Youth Service America, 1992.

Torbet, Patricia McFall. *A Special Report on Juvenile Crack Dealers*. Pittsburgh, PA: National Center for Juvenile Justice, 1992.

Weiner, Neil Allan, and Wolfgang, Marvin E., eds. *Pathways to Criminal Violence*. Newbury Park, CA: Sage Publications, 1989.

Weisheit, Ralph A., and Culbertson, Robert G. *Juvenile Delinquency: A Justice Perspective*. Prospect Heights, IL: Waveland Press, 1985.

Whitcomb, Debra. *When the Victim Is a Child*. Washington, D.C.: National Institute of Justice, 1992.

Wooden, Kenneth. *Weeping in the Playtime of Others*. New York: McGraw-Hill, 1976.

Yochelson, Samuel, and Samenow, Stanton. *The Criminal Personality: A Profile for Change*, Vol. I. New York: Jason Aronson, 1976.

———. *The Criminal Personality*, Vol. III. Northvale, NJ: Jason Aronson, 1986.

Index

Index

Index

Index

Index